BEYOND THE VOICE

The Inspiring Life and Legacy of James Earl Jones

Natty Mann

COPYRIGHT

DISCLAIMER

This biography is an independent publication that has been meticulously researched to provide a comprehensive account of the life and experiences of the individual in focus.

It is not affiliated with any official organization, institution, or entity associated with the subject.

The information presented in this book is derived from a variety of sources, including historical records, interviews, and publicly available materials.

While every effort has been made to ensure accuracy, the content is the result of an independent research endeavor and should be considered as such.

Readers are encouraged to verify and cross-reference information found within this biography, especially regarding specific historical events, dates, or details.

The author and publisher do not claim any official endorsement or authorization from the subject or their representatives, and this work is not intended to serve as an official biography.

This biography is a testament to the dedication and passion of independent authors and researchers who strive to shed light on the lives and legacies of remarkable individuals.

It is offered to the public as a unique perspective on the subject and is intended for informational and educational purposes.

Thank you for being so understanding, and we hope you find this independent biography insightful and engaging.

CONTENTS

CHAPTER 1

EARLY YEARS

Childhood in Mississippi

James Earl Jones was born on January 17, 1931, in Arkabutla, Mississippi, a small community woven into the rich cultural jumble of the American South. James, the son of actor Robert Earl Jones and actress Ruth Connolly, was involved in performing from a young age. However, his youth was shaped by the arts and the period's racial difficulties and socioeconomic challenges. Growing up in a segregated culture, he witnessed directly the terrible realities of discrimination, which shaped his perspective and artistic expression.

Living in a remote area, young James found peace in the natural beauty around him—rolling hills, huge fields, and the sounds of the Mississippi Delta. These aspects would subsequently permeate his work, instilling a great love for storytelling and the complexities of human experience. However, despite this magnificent environment, he encountered enormous challenges that molded his identity.

Struggles with Stuttering

James had a terrible stammer from a young age, making communication difficult. Words frequently eluded him, causing frustration and loneliness. In a world where expression was essential, his speech impairment felt like a wall between him and others around him. This battle was more than just a personal difficulty; it was a deep source of grief that would follow him throughout his formative years.

In school, he grew acutely aware of how his stammer distinguished him from his peers. The laughter and mockery from classmates exacerbated his sense of inadequacy, forcing him deeper into silence. During these times of isolation, he discovered the power of listening—a talent that would eventually help him improve his acting profession. He began to appreciate the beauty of written language and spent much time reading literature and poetry.

The Role of Family and Education

Despite the difficulties he encountered, James found steadfast support from his family. His mother, a teacher, saw his challenges and encouraged him to express himself via writing and acting. She introduced him to Shakespeare and classic literature, laying the groundwork for a lifetime love of storytelling. His father, despite being less present during his upbringing, instilled in him a feeling of pride in his lineage and the value of endurance.

Jones initially enrolled at the University of Michigan as a pre-med student but eventually decided to study acting instead. After graduating, he served in the military during the Korean War before pursuing a career in acting.

Education was extremely important in James' development. After traveling to Michigan to live with his mother, he attended a new school where he met professors who saw his potential. One teacher in particular expressed an interest in developing his acting abilities. Through drama workshops and school productions, James discovered his voice—not only as a speaker but also as an artist. The theater became a haven for him to overcome his stutter and express emotions and storylines that words alone could not.

As he navigated the complications of childhood, James Earl Jones emerged not only as a young man dealing with personal issues but also as someone ready to embrace the transforming potential of art. This phase of his life established the groundwork for the incredible adventure that would lead him to become one of the most legendary voices in film and theater.

CHAPTER 2

DISCOVERING THE VOICE

James Earl Jones' journey to establishing his legendary voice was both about the art of theatre and about personal development. From his first performances on stage to the difficulties he encountered, each step added to the tremendous resonance that would define his career. This chapter delves into the enormous impact of theatre on Jones' life, the challenges he faced, and the first steps he took in his acting career.

The Influence of Theatre

For James Earl Jones, the theatre was a haven—a place where he could explore his identity and express feelings that were frequently overpowering in the real world. Jones found consolation in the realm of drama after growing up in a turbulent environment and suffering from a stammer throughout his early childhood. It was here that he could turn his struggles into art.

Theatre has always been a medium for narrative, and Jones used it to reclaim his voice. He learned that by creating characters, he could express emotions and narratives that resonated deeply with him. Each role helped to explore different aspects of humanity, such as love, grief, courage, and vulnerability.

Jones took part in performances during high school, which sparked his interest in acting. He immersed himself in the works of Shakespeare and other playwrights, realizing that these stories were more than just scripts, but also reflections of the human experience. The stage allowed him to explore complicated ideas while honing his technique.

Theatre is intrinsically collaborative, requiring actors to collaborate closely with directors, co-stars, and production crews. Jones believed that teamwork was critical to developing confidence and resilience. He learned the value of listening—both to the text and to his co-stars. This focus not only improved his performance but also created a sense of camaraderie.

As he learned the complexities of ensemble work, Jones realized that theatre was a communal experience. The energy transferred between actors and audiences created an electrifying atmosphere that drove his enthusiasm for performing. This sense of belonging inspired him to pursue performing despite the obstacles he faced.

Jones' relationship with his voice shifted as he began performing. Each time he took the stage, he battled his stutter, directing his energy into the roles he played. The act of performing became a type of catharsis, allowing people to transcend their constraints and connect with others on a deeper level.

Jones realized a new sense of liberation when he allowed himself to be fully present in a part. The stage became a place where he could express himself freely without fear of being judged. This liberation would eventually inspire him to embrace his voice as a tool for power and influence.

Overcoming Challenges

Despite his evident talent, James Earl Jones encountered numerous hurdles on his way to becoming one of the world's most famous voices. These challenges developed his personality and resilience.

Jones was plagued by the anxiety of being vulnerable. His stutter had long been a source of anxiety, causing an internal conflict between his need to speak and his fear of being misunderstood. The stage provided a paradox: it was both an outlet for emotion and a source of worry.

To overcome this dread, Jones leaned into the personas he played. He realized that by immersing himself in their experiences, he could get past his insecurities. This adjustment in perspective enabled him to see vulnerability as a strength rather than a weakness. As he played many roles, he realized that genuineness resonated more deeply than perfection.

Rejection is an unavoidable aspect of every artistic endeavor, and Jones knows personally. Early auditions frequently failed, leading him to doubt his ability. Rather than surrendering to despair, he turned rejection into fuel for growth.

Each setback led him to reflect and develop himself. Jones solicited feedback from mentors and peers, knowing that constructive criticism was crucial for improving his trade. This resilience became a defining feature of his character—an unflinching determination to overcome hardship.

As an artist aspiring for excellence, Jones struggled with self-criticism. The pressure to meet high standards bore heavily on him, especially as he began to be recognized for his abilities. However, he learned the value of balancing self-criticism and self-compassion.

Jones developed a more positive inner dialogue through mindfulness practices and reflection. He accepted that mistakes were a part of the learning process and saw them as opportunities for improvement. This transition enabled him to approach acting with renewed joy rather than dread, a critical transformation that would serve him well throughout his career.

First Steps in Acting

James Earl Jones' first steps into the field of acting were defined by curiosity and commitment. These formative encounters paved the way for a wonderful career.

Jones' academic path had a significant impact on his acting abilities. After attending the University of Michigan, he engaged himself in theatre studies, performing in a variety of shows that helped him to hone his craft. This formal education gave him vital tools such as vocal training, movement exercises, and a knowledge of dramatic literature.

Jones found community theatre to be an invaluable resource for his acting development. He took part in local productions, which allowed him to experiment with new parts and techniques without the pressure of professional expectations. These encounters built friendships among other actors and fueled his passion for storytelling.

Recognizing the benefits of mentorship, Jones sought advice from seasoned actors and directors who might share industry expertise. Their guidance helped him overcome obstacles and have a better knowledge of character work. This coaching was crucial in developing both confidence and skill.

Jones knew that his voice was essential to his craft, so he practiced vocal exercises to improve his articulation and breath control. He developed daily practices to improve his voice range and clarity, transforming what had previously been a source of insecurity into a tool of strength.

Improv became an essential part of Jones' training. Improvisational exercises let him think swiftly on his feet and respond truthfully to unforeseen situations. This versatility led to better stage performances, allowing him to connect more profoundly with both characters and audiences.

Jones' passion for literature went beyond screenplays; he studied many genres and writers to enhance his understanding of storytelling strategies. Reading plays from many cultures and times broadened his view on character development and story structure, sparking his inventiveness as an actor.

Jones actively solicited comments from directors and colleagues after performances, promoting ongoing learning. He saw constructive criticism as an opportunity for growth, not as a sign of inadequacy. This openness helped him to grow as an actor while also strengthening his relationship with the subject.

Above all, James Earl Jones seized every chance that came his way, no matter how tiny. Whether it was a little role in a play or a television audition, he embraced each opportunity with passion and dedication. This determination paved the way for future success.

The influence of theatre shaped James Earl Jones' journey to developing his voice, including the stories he told, the connections he made, and the problems he faced. Through vulnerability, resilience, and relentless dedication to his work, he turned challenges into stepping stones to greatness. As we progress through his life in later chapters, we will see how these early experiences paved the way for one of the most legendary voices in entertainment history.

CHAPTER 3

BREAKING THROUGH

James Earl Jones's ascent in the world of acting was not an overnight phenomenon; it was a gradual process marked by determination, talent, and a series of pivotal performances that showcased his remarkable range. This chapter delves into his early roles, the transformative impact of Broadway, and his eventual transition to film and television—each step solidifying his place in the entertainment industry.

Early Performances and Roles

In the early stages of his career, James Earl Jones took on a variety of roles that allowed him to hone his craft and develop his unique voice. His first significant break came with his performance in the off-Broadway play ***"The Blacks"*** in 1961. The production, which explored themes of race and identity, provided Jones with an opportunity to showcase his powerful presence on stage. Critics praised his ability to convey deep emotion, and this role marked a turning point in his career.

Jones was acutely aware of the limited opportunities available to Black actors during the 1960s. He sought out diverse roles that challenged stereotypes and offered nuanced portrayals of African American experiences. His commitment to authenticity resonated with audiences and critics alike, leading to more prominent opportunities.

In 1963, Jones starred in ***"The Long Dream"***, a play by African American playwright Alice Childress. This role allowed him to delve into complex themes of race and personal struggle. His performance was met with acclaim, further establishing him as a formidable talent in the theatre community.

As he continued to take on challenging roles, Jones built a reputation as a versatile actor. He appeared in various productions, including ***"Othello"***, where he portrayed the titular character with a depth that captivated audiences. His interpretation of Othello was groundbreaking, as he brought a unique perspective to the role, blending vulnerability with strength.

These early performances paved the way for a prosperous career. Each role contributed to his growing confidence and mastery of the craft, preparing him for the next phase of his journey.

The Impact of Broadway

Broadway would become a defining chapter in James Earl Jones's career. His debut on the Great White Way in *"The Great White Hope"* in 1968 marked a significant milestone. The play, which addressed racial tensions through the lens of boxing, resonated deeply with audiences and critics alike.

Jones's portrayal of Jack Johnson, the first African American heavyweight boxing champion, was both powerful and poignant. He infused the character with a sense of dignity while navigating the complexities of race relations in America. The role earned him critical acclaim and solidified his status as a leading man on Broadway.

The success of *"The Great White Hope"* led to a Tony Award for Best Actor in a Play, making Jones one of the few Black actors to receive such recognition at that time. This achievement not only validated his talent but also opened doors for future generations of Black performers.

The experience of performing on Broadway was transformative for Jones. The energy of a live audience fueled his performances, allowing him to connect with spectators in a way that felt electric. Each standing ovation reinforced his belief in the power of storytelling and the importance of representation on stage.

During this time, Jones also had the opportunity to collaborate with renowned directors and fellow actors who challenged him creatively. These collaborations enriched his understanding of character development and heightened his appreciation for the art form.

Following the success of *"The Great White Hope"*, Jones continued to take on diverse roles on Broadway, including *"Fences"* by August Wilson. This powerful drama explored themes of family, race, and regret—elements that resonated deeply with Jones' own experiences. His performance garnered rave reviews and further established him as one of the most respected actors in the industry.

Transition to Film and Television

As Jones' reputation grew on Broadway, so did interest from Hollywood. The transition from stage to screen presented both opportunities and challenges, but Jones approached it with the same dedication that had characterized his theatrical work.

Jones made his film debut in 1969 with *"The Great White Hope"*, reprising his acclaimed stage role for the big screen. This transition was seamless; he brought the same intensity and depth to his performance that had captivated Broadway audiences. The film further showcased his ability to convey complex emotions through subtle gestures and vocal nuances.

In the years that followed, Jones took on a variety of film roles that highlighted his versatility. He starred in *"Dr. Strangelove or: How I Learned to Stop Worrying and Love the Bomb"* (1964), where he played a military officer—a role that showcased his ability to navigate both drama and dark comedy.

As Jones transitioned into television, he continued to break barriers. His portrayal of Alex Haley in the landmark miniseries ***"Roots"*** (1977) was groundbreaking. The series chronicled the history of African Americans from slavery to freedom, and Jones' performance was pivotal in bringing this important narrative to life. His work resonated deeply with audiences and helped elevate discussions about race in America.

This role not only garnered critical acclaim but also earned him an Emmy Award nomination—further solidifying his status as a versatile actor capable of tackling socially relevant themes.

Voice Work and Iconic Characters

One of Jones' most iconic contributions came through voice work. His deep, resonant voice became synonymous with authority and gravitas. He lent his voice to numerous documentaries and narrations, including Disney's ***"The Lion King"***, where he voiced Mufasa—a role that introduced him to a new generation of fans.

Jones embraced these opportunities wholeheartedly, understanding that voice work was an extension of his craft. He brought the same emotional depth to these projects as he did on stage or screen—transforming characters into unforgettable figures.

As James Earl Jones transitioned from stage to screen, he not only broke through barriers for himself but also paved the way for future generations of actors. His commitment to authenticity and representation resonated throughout the industry, inspiring others to embrace their voices and stories.

James Earl Jones's journey through early performances, Broadway triumphs, and successful transitions into film and television exemplifies resilience and artistry. Each step marked a breakthrough—an opportunity to redefine what it meant to be a Black actor in America. As we move forward in this narrative, we will explore how these experiences shaped not only his career but also his legacy as one of the most celebrated voices in entertainment history.

CHAPTER 4

ICONIC ROLES

James Earl Jones' career is defined by a string of remarkable performances that have left an indelible impression on both stage and screen. This chapter looks into some of his most iconic performances, such as the frightening Darth Vader, the noble Mufasa, and other notable characters who demonstrate his incredible versatility and talent. Each role showcases Jones' distinct abilities while simultaneously emphasizing the cultural relevance of his contributions to the arts.

Darth Vader: The Voice of a Villain

In 1977, George Lucas's ***"Star Wars"*** premiered, introducing audiences to a galaxy far, far away—and to one of cinema's most iconic villains: Darth Vader. While the character was initially portrayed physically by David Prowse, it was Jones's deep, commanding voice that brought Vader to life. His vocal performance transformed the character into a symbol of fear and authority, resonating with audiences worldwide.

Jones approached the role with a distinct methodology. He infused Vader with a sense of gravitas, using his rich baritone to convey power and menace. In the recording booth, he experimented with different vocal inflections and tones, ultimately settling on a delivery that was both chilling and authoritative. This meticulous attention to detail made Vader not just a villain, but a complex character whose presence loomed large over the *"Star Wars"* saga.

Darth Vader quickly became a pop culture phenomenon, transcending the boundaries of film. The character's iconic breathing sound and memorable lines—such as "I am your father"—have become ingrained in the collective consciousness. Jones' portrayal has influenced countless subsequent villains in film and television, establishing a benchmark for how powerful voices can shape characters.

Jones reprised his role as Darth Vader in several sequels and spin-offs, including *"The Empire Strikes Back"* (1980), *"Return of the Jedi"* (1983), and the prequel trilogy. Each return added layers to the character, allowing audiences to explore Vader's complexities and vulnerabilities. Jones's commitment to the role ensured that Darth Vader remained a central figure in the ***"Star Wars"*** universe, solidifying his legacy as one of cinema's most memorable characters.

Mufasa: A Legacy in Animation

Disney produced "The Lion King" in 1994, a pioneering animated film that has since become a beloved classic. James Earl Jones voiced Mufasa, the wise and noble lion who acted as both father and king. This part was the turning point in Jones' career, demonstrating his ability to connect emotionally with people of all ages.

Jones handled Mufasa with the same passion that he had shown in all of his previous roles. He filled the character with warmth and power, and his voice conveyed both strength and tenderness. Mufasa's renowned remarks, such as "Remember who you are," are spoken with such gravitas that they strike a deep chord with viewers, teaching essential lessons about identity and responsibility.

Mufasa's character goes beyond mere animation; he embodies concepts of leadership, sacrifice, and familial devotion. The film's examination of the circle of life strikes a chord with audiences all across the world, cementing Mufasa's legacy as a symbol of wisdom and leadership. Jones' depiction helped the character become a cultural icon, inspiring generations of admirers.

Jones returns to voice Mufasa in Disney's live-action remake of "The Lion King" in 2019, cementing his bond with the character. His reprisal not only demonstrated his timeless talent but also established Mufasa's status in popular culture as a symbol of strength and virtue.

Other Memorable Characters

While Darth Vader and Mufasa are among Jones' most iconic roles, his career has featured a varied range of characters that demonstrate his ability as an actor. Jones has played a variety of roles ranging from drama to comedy, highlighting diverse aspects of his talents.

The King in "The Great White Hope"

Revisiting his theatrical roots, Jones' portrayal of Jack Johnson in "The Great White Hope" remains one of his most powerful performances. The job allowed him to explore themes of racial identity and cultural expectations in early twentieth-century America. His performance received critical acclaim and demonstrated his ability to handle difficult roles with depth and sensitivity.

The Wise Mentor in "Field of Dreams"

Jones portrays Terence Mann, a reclusive author who becomes a mentor to Kevin Costner's character, in the 1989 film "Field of Dreams". His portrayal caught Mann's knowledge and tenderness, lending emotional weight to the story. The film's study of aspirations, redemption, and father-son connections hit home with audiences, cementing Jones' reputation as a brilliant storyteller.

A Voice for Justice in "The Sandlot"

In "The Sandlot" (1993), Jones plays Mr. Mertle, a mysterious character who becomes an odd mentor to a group of young boys. His role acts as a bridge across generations, teaching important lessons about friendship and teamwork. This role demonstrated Jones' ability to connect with younger audiences while still conveying serious truths.

The Narrator: A Voice for Documentaries

Jones has voiced various documentaries and narrations, including PBS's "The Civil War" and National Geographic specials. His resonant voice lends weight to historical storytelling, making complex subjects more approachable and intriguing for audiences. Through his work, he has established himself as a renowned voice in instructional programming.

James Earl Jones' legendary roles as Darth Vader, Mufasa, and others demonstrate his incredible ability to bring characters to life across multiple genres. His efforts have entertained and inspired audiences all around the world. As we continue to follow Jones' journey in later chapters, it becomes evident that his legacy is characterized not just by the characters he has played, but also by the enormous impact he has had on the arts and society as a whole. His voice has resonated across decades, reminding us all of the power of narrative.

CHAPTER 5

HIS ART OF PERFORMANCE

Techniques and Training

His early encounters with speech difficulties prompted him to explore the power of voice and words. Encouraged by a supportive teacher, he began to view acting as a form of self-expression. This formative phase was critical, as it taught him the value of clarity and control in performance.

Jones studied acting at the University of Michigan and received a Bachelor of Arts degree. His university studies gave him with a good foundation in classical theatre, exposing him to a wide spectrum of styles from Shakespearean performance to contemporary American drama. This diversified training provided him with the tools he needed to handle numerous tasks throughout his career.

While Jones has frequently used parts of method acting, he has established an own approach that combines emotional sincerity with vocal precision. He believes in thoroughly comprehending a character's motivations and backstory, which allows him to truly enter parts. This attention to character development is reflected in his performances, which frequently convey a palpable feeling of honesty and depth.

Jones saw the potential of his voice as an instrument and committed time in voice training. He studied vocal techniques that focused on breath control, resonance, and projection. This technique enabled him to fully realize the power of his baritone voice, allowing him to portray a wide range of emotions, from Darth Vader's imposing authority to Mufasa's maternal wisdom. His dedication to vocal excellence has distinguished him in an industry where the voice can make or break a performance.

The Power of Voice in Acting

James Earl Jones' voice is one of his most distinguishing features. Its deep timbre and rich resonance have made it instantly recognizable, allowing him to create characters that audiences remember long after the credits have rolled. His voice is more than just a medium of communication; it is also an effective tool for emotional expression.

Jones recognizes that voice carries emotional weight. He meticulously adjusts his tone to capture the intricacies of each character he plays. Mufasa's voice in *The Lion King*, for example, embodies the characteristics of a loving father and a wise king while also conveying authority. Jones' ability to generate emotion through voice is a defining feature of his performances, creating an indelible impression on audiences.

In addition to vocal delivery, Jones understands the value of quiet in performance. Pauses may be as effective as words, allowing moments to breathe and giving spectators time to process the weight of a situation. His intentional use of quiet heightens dramatic tension, making key moments even more poignant.

Aside from character parts, Jones' voice has found a home in narration. His work on documentaries and instructional television demonstrates his ability to captivate audiences with storytelling. The gravitas he contributes to these projects gives historical narratives authority, making complex topics more accessible and appealing.

Collaborations with Directors and Actors

Throughout his career, James Earl Jones has worked with some of the most renowned directors in film and on stage. His ability to adapt to numerous styles while preserving his distinctive voice has made him a popular actor for a variety of projects.

One of Jones' most well-known collaborations was with director George Lucas on the "Star Wars" trilogy. Lucas realized the significance of voice in establishing Darth Vader's commanding presence. Their collaboration demonstrates how a director's vision may be enhanced by an actor's performance. Jones' rendition of Vader added dimension to the character, converting him from a simple villain to a complicated figure whose troubles resonate with fans.

Jones' experience with Disney on "The Lion King" allowed him to collaborate with brilliant animators and directors who recognized the importance of voice in animation. His meetings with directors such as Roger Allers and Rob Minkoff demonstrated the value of collaboration between voice acting and visual narrative. Together, they created sequences that flawlessly combined animation and vocal performance.

Jones has also collaborated with several renowned performers, resulting in dynamic ensemble casts that improve storytelling. In films such as "Field of Dreams," he starred with Kevin Costner, bringing out the best in each other's performances. His ability to listen and respond sincerely to fellow performers enhances every scene he appears in, generating a sense of reality that captivates audiences.

Jones, a seasoned performer, has taken on a teaching role for newer actors. He knows the hurdles that rising talent faces and frequently gives advice gleaned from his own experiences. His eagerness to collaborate and encourage others demonstrates his dedication to promoting creativity in the profession.

The art of performing is a complex quilt created through training, technique, and teamwork. James

Earl Jones personifies this artistry through his mastery of voice and ability to connect profoundly with characters. His journey from overcoming personal obstacles to becoming one of the most renowned characters in the industry serves as an example to budding actors everywhere. As we continue to investigate his legacy in future chapters, we will see how these artistic ideas affected not only his career but also the landscape of modern acting.

CHAPTER 6

PERSONAL LIFE

James Earl Jones' life away from the stage and screen is as diverse and rich as his performances. This chapter looks into his relationships and family, his efforts to balance fame and privacy, and his dedication to philanthropy and advocacy. Each facet portrays the man behind the renowned voice, emphasizing his ideals and the concepts that govern him.

Relationships and Family

James Earl Jones was born to Robert Earl Jones, an actor and boxer, and Ruth Connolly, a teacher. His parents' division when he was a child had a significant impact on him. He was mostly raised by his mother in Michigan. Despite this, his mother instilled in him a strong sense of self-esteem and the value of education.

Jones' personal life has entailed two significant marriages. His first marriage was to Julienne Marie, an actress and singer, in 1966. The pair had a passion for the arts, but their relationship was short-lived, ending in divorce in 1972.

Jones married Cecilia Hart, a well-known stage and television actress, in 1982. Their friendship grew into a strong relationship that lasted until Hart died in 2016. The couple had one son, Flynn Earl Jones, who was born in 1982. Flynn has followed in his father's footsteps by seeking a career in the arts.

Jones has repeatedly discussed the joys and hardships of fatherhood. He has shown delight in raising Flynn and ensuring that he obtained a comprehensive education. Jones' experiences as a father informed his approach to characters like Mufasa in **"The Lion King"**, where themes of guidance and protection are vividly felt. He has underlined the importance of developing children's creativity and encouraging them to pursue their passions.

Balancing Fame and Privacy

As one of the world's most famous voices, James Earl Jones has handled the complications of fame with grace. He is well aware of the public's obsession with celebrity culture but has always emphasized his privacy. Unlike numerous actors who enjoy the spotlight, Jones has decided to keep a quiet profile outside of his professional career.

Jones has been choosy in his public appearances and his interactions with the media. He rarely engages in tabloid culture or sensationalism, preferring to focus on his profession. This decision has enabled him to develop an image characterized by respect and admiration rather than scandal or controversy. In interviews, he frequently emphasizes the value of honesty over public impression.

Jones' philosophy focuses on humility and thankfulness. He understands that popularity may be ephemeral and that genuine fulfillment stems from meaningful connections rather than public accolades. His grounded attitude shines through in how he interacts with fans; he is noted for being approachable and kind during interactions, frequently taking the time to engage with individuals who appreciate his work.

Philanthropy and Advocacy

James Earl Jones has been a lifelong promoter of education. He understands the transforming potential of learning, having experienced it as a student with speech impairments. He has supported several educational projects that attempt to provide chances for impoverished youth.

Jones founded the James Earl Jones Scholarship Fund at the University of Michigan in 1990 to help students pursue degrees in theater and performing arts. His dedication to developing emerging talent reflects his desire to give back to the community that helped mold him.

Jones' involvement goes beyond schooling; he has been involved in civil rights activities. He marched in the civil rights movement of the 1960s, utilizing his voice to speak out against injustice and unfairness. His involvement demonstrates his belief in the value of social justice and equality for all people.

Jones, a renowned artist, has promoted the arts through a variety of organizations. He has served on the boards of organizations such as the Actors Studio and has been involved in efforts aimed at increasing diversity in theater and movies. His services have helped to establish spaces for aspiring artists from various backgrounds to tell their tales.

In recent years, Jones has also become an environmental activist. He has spoken out in support of sustainability and conservation measures, acknowledging the importance of environmental protection for future generations. His participation demonstrates his dedication to not only social issues but also global challenges that affect mankind as a whole.

James Earl Jones' personal life exemplifies a strong devotion to family, privacy, and civic duty. His interactions shaped him into the person he is today: an artist who values connection, authenticity, and service to others. As we study his legacy in later chapters, we will see how these personal ideals informed his professional choices and led to his long-lasting impact on both the arts and society as a whole.

CHAPTER 7

AWARDS AND RECOGNITION

James Earl Jones' lengthy career has been marked by various accolades and medals that recognize his exceptional talent and contributions to the arts. This chapter dives into his accolades, his tremendous cultural impact, and the legacy he is leaving for future generations of artists.

Major Awards and Honors

While James Earl Jones has never won an Academy Award, he has been nominated for his outstanding performance in "The Great White Hope" (1970). His performance as boxer Jack Johnson was pioneering, demonstrating his ability to inhabit complicated characters with depth and sensitivity. The movie not only gained him critical acclaim but also cemented his reputation as a formidable figure in Hollywood.

Jones' theatrical abilities have garnered him two Tony Awards. The first came in 1969 for his performance in "The Great White Hope," making him one of the few

African American actors to garner such accolades at the time. His second Tony came in 1987 for August Wilson's epic drama "Fences," which examines issues of racism, family, and personal struggle. Both performances showcased his ability to express real passion and authenticity on stage.

In addition to his theatrical accomplishments, Jones has received attention on television. He received an Emmy Award in 1991 for his work in the miniseries *Heat Wave*, demonstrating his flexibility as an actor in several disciplines. This award solidified his status as a household name and honored his contributions to television storytelling.

Jones' contributions to the arts have been recognized with several lifetime achievement awards. In 2017, he earned the coveted Screen Actors Guild Life Achievement Award, which recognized his accomplishments in the performing industry and community service. This honor recognizes not only his artistic achievements but also his position as a mentor and advocate for other artists.

In appreciation of his artistic accomplishments and humanitarian activities, President Barack Obama awarded James Earl Jones the National Medal of Arts in 2012. This prize is one of the greatest accolades bestowed upon artists in the United States, honoring individuals who have made major contributions to American culture.

Contributions to Arts and Culture

Jones has long been a forerunner for African American representation in the arts. His works in film, television, and theatre have paved the way for future generations of actors of color. By portraying multifaceted individuals who defy preconceptions, he has encouraged the industry to value diversity and honesty in storytelling.

Jones' unique voice has become associated with various classic characters, most notably Darth Vader in the "Star Wars" trilogy and Mufasa in "The Lion King" His ability to express authority, gravitas, and emotional depth solely through voice has transformed the field of voice acting. These roles have had a lasting impact on popular culture, influencing how characters are portrayed and evolved in animation and film.

Aside from his performances, Jones has actively mentored young actors and artists. He has shared his knowledge and experiences through seminars, interviews, and public speaking appearances, highlighting the value of hard effort, discipline, and honesty in the arts. His support for diversity in casting and narrative continues to inspire new talent to pursue their goals courageously.

Impact on Future Generations

James Earl Jones' journey from a stuttering youngster to an accomplished actor is a source of inspiration for aspiring artists. His story demonstrates how perseverance and devotion may help you overcome problems. Many young actors consider him a big influence in their lives, citing his performances as sparking their interest in acting.

Jones' scholarship fund at the University of Michigan, as well as other educational efforts, have had a direct impact on the lives of numerous students pursuing arts careers. He contributes to the development of a new generation of diverse voices in theatre and film by giving financial support and mentorship opportunities.

Jones' contributions go beyond individual performances; they are part of a larger cultural heritage that promotes representation and inclusion. His work has set the path for tales that reflect the breadth of human experience from many perspectives. As society evolves, his impact inspires storytellers to explore topics such as identity, perseverance, and social justice.

As future generations reflect on the world of American theatre and film, James Earl Jones will be remembered as a crucial person who altered the industry. His dedication to sincerity, support for diversity, and unmatched talent have set a standard that many people strive to meet.

CHAPTER 8

HIS LEGACY

As James Earl Jones's incredible career ends, it is important to reflect on the deep legacy he left behind. This chapter explores his impact on modern acting, the cultural significance of his work, and genuine reactions from contemporaries and fans whose talents have moved.

Influence on Modern Acting

James Earl Jones has not only changed the face of acting, but he has also reinvented what it means to be an actor in today's world. His transformation from a stuttering child to a stage and movie legend is a lesson in perseverance and determination.

Jones' ability to depict multidimensional personalities has motivated many performers to take on roles that violate societal standards and expectations. His performances have inspired a generation to go deeper into their profession, forcing them to investigate the emotional complexities of their characters. In a field that is frequently chastised for typecasting, Jones has demonstrated that great talent transcends color, background, and even vocal restrictions.

One of the most important lessons current actors may take from Jones is the art of presence. Whether commanding the stage in a Broadway production or contributing his voice to an animated classic, he has an incredible capacity to capture viewers with a simple quiet or a subtle shift in tone. This knowledge of presence teaches prospective actors that sometimes less is more, and that the weight of a moment can be felt strongly without saying a single word.

Jones' influence goes beyond his performances; he regularly mentors aspiring actors, giving his knowledge and views. His dedication to developing talent reflects his idea that the future of acting lies in collaboration and assistance. In workshops and interviews, he emphasizes the value of authenticity, urging young artists to discover their voices rather than adapt to business standards.

Cultural Significance of His Work

James Earl Jones' accomplishments are embedded in the very fabric of American civilization. His art goes beyond entertainment, sparking discussions about race, identity, and humanity.

Jones has been a forerunner for African American actors at an age when representation is crucial. His roles have challenged prejudices and provided opportunities for diverse storytelling. He has brought depth and dignity to characters that reflect the richness of the African American experience, from Jack Johnson in "The Great White Hope" to Mufasa in "The Lion King". His presence on television and on stage has motivated filmmakers and writers to tell stories that celebrate diversity and include perspectives from all walks of life.

Jones' distinctive voice has become synonymous with authority and wisdom. As Darth Vader, he not only brought a villain to life but also turned him into a cultural figure. This role revealed that even antagonists can be multifaceted and intriguing, forcing audiences to reassess their perceptions of good and evil. His performance has affected other filmmakers and voice actors, who aim to achieve the same level of seriousness in their work.

Many of Jones' performances include a stinging social critique. In plays such as "Fences," he explores themes of race, family, and personal struggle that resonate with audiences of all ages. His ability to elicit empathy through storytelling encourages audiences to discuss tough themes, resulting in a better knowledge of societal concerns.

Reflections from Peers and Fans

As we explore James Earl Jones' legacy, we must hear from individuals who have walked beside him or been inspired by his work. Friends, coworkers, and admirers alike discuss what makes him such an iconic presence in the arts.

Renowned actors such as Denzel Washington and Viola Davis have frequently discussed Jones' influence on their careers. Washington once said, "James Earl Jones is a masterclass in acting." He showed me that power is found not in loudness, but in stillness." Davis agrees, underlining how Jones' genuineness inspires others to see their vulnerabilities as virtues.

Directors such as George Lucas have acknowledged their appreciation for Jones' contributions. Lucas referred to him as "the voice of a generation," emphasizing how his portrayal of Darth Vader provided depths to the character that went beyond the screenplay. For many filmmakers, casting Jones means elevating a project's artistic integrity.

For fans throughout the world, James Earl Jones is more than just an actor; he is a cultural icon. Many people remember seeing "Star Wars" or "The Lion King" as children and being captivated by his voice and presence. Fans have paid tribute to him on social media, sharing personal anecdotes of how his performances touched them at key points in their lives.

One admirer wrote, "Listening to Mufasa's remarks about the circle of life helped me manage my issues with loss. It felt like he was speaking directly to me." Such views demonstrate how Jones' work has had a far-reaching impact on people, serving as a source of comfort and inspiration.

As we gather these views, it becomes evident that James Earl Jones left a diverse legacy. He is not just an actor, but also a mentor, a supporter of representation, and a source of inspiration for young artists. His legacy will last through generations, motivating young storytellers to embrace their craft with passion and authenticity.

James Earl Jones left a legacy of resilience, representation, and deep artistry. His impact on modern acting is evident; he has established a level of sincerity that resonates strongly inside the business. His art is culturally meaningful in ways that go beyond amusement, and it invites us to reflect on our shared humanity.

As we reflect on his journey, we celebrate not only his accomplishments but also the lasting impression he has made on our hearts and minds. In every performance and position he has taken on, James Earl Jones reminds us that stories—and the voices that tell them—are important. As we move forward, we carry on his legacy of encouraging everyone to find their voices and tell their stories with courage and elegance.

Thoughts on Aging and Career Longevity

As James Earl Jones approached the end of his career, he faced aging with elegance and wisdom. In interviews, he frequently comments on the lessons learned over decades in the industry and how they have shaped his approach to both life and work.

"Aging is not something to fear; it is an opportunity to evolve," he says, with a sparkle in his eye. Each year, Jones gains new viewpoints and ideas that improve his performance. He sees aging as a blessing, an opportunity to delve deeper into the complexities of personality and emotion. "With age comes experience, and experience is vital," he maintains."

Many of those who have witnessed his artistic development agree with his philosophy. Rather than shying away from roles that reflect his age, Jones seeks characters who represent the intricacies of life at all stages. This technique not only violates Hollywood clichés about aging performers, but it also provides audiences with a more authentic portrayal of the human condition.

Jones emphasized the significance of self-care in extending one's career. He opened up about the physical difficulties of acting and how staying active—both mentally and physically—has been critical for him. "I have learned that taking care of my body is just as important as honing my craft," the artist says. Regular exercise, meditation, and a well-balanced diet have become part of his daily routine, allowing him to stay active and interested at work.

His optimistic attitude about aging serves as an example to many others who are dealing with societal constraints associated with getting older. He inspires others to embrace each chapter of their lives with zest.

His Death

James Earl Jones died on September 9, 2024, at the age of 93, signaling the end of a truly famous career in entertainment.

EPILOGUE

A Voice That Shaped Generations

Few voices in film and theatre resound as deeply as James Earl Jones'. His rich, resonant tones have not only defined characters but also sculpted the fabric of narrative throughout decades. As we reflect on Jones' incredible career, it becomes clear that his legacy goes far beyond the roles he played; it is ingrained in the hearts and minds of audiences all across the world.

A Legacy of Iconic Roles

From his iconic performance as Mufasa in "The Lion King" to his dominating presence as Darth Vader in "Star Wars", Jones' performances transcend time and genre. His voice has become linked with authority and wisdom, exuding gravitas that few can match. These great performances have not only delighted millions, but have also provoked debates about identity, power, and morality.

Mufasa: A Father Figure for All Ages.

Mufasa, the wise and noble lion, is one of Jones' favorite characters. His voice gives the character a warmth and strength that appeals to audiences of all ages. Mufasa's lessons on responsibility, courage, and the circle of life have become timeless teachings for families all across the world. The emotional power of his words—"Remember who you are"—has inspired countless people to embrace their genuine selves and conduct their journeys with integrity.

Darth Vader: The Complexity of Villainy

Jones, on the other hand, portrays Darth Vader as a nuanced adversary. His deep, threatening voice made Vader an iconic emblem of terror and authority. However, beneath that tough demeanor lies a terrible story of loss and redemption. Jones used this figure to explore themes of conflict and development, urging the spectator to confront the duality of human nature. The legendary remark, "I am your father," is one of cinema's most impactful moments, forever changing the face of film storytelling.

Impacting Future Generations

Beyond particular roles, James Earl Jones has had an immense impact on future generations of performers and filmmakers. His devotion to craft and commitment to honesty serve as a beacon for budding artists navigating the often turbulent waters of the entertainment business.

A Mentor and Inspiration

Jones' mentorship extends beyond official programs; it is integrated into the fabric of his relationships with emerging talent. He has frequently made time to speak with aspiring performers, imparting insights gained from his career. His emphasis on hard effort, resilience, and the value of storytelling resonates emotionally with individuals who want to follow in his footsteps. Many people have cited him as an inspiration, seeing his encouragement as a spur for their artistic endeavors.

Breaking Barriers

Jones has been a trailblazer his whole career, breaking down barriers for Black actors in Hollywood. His breakthrough has cleared the way for more representation in film and theater, challenging preconceptions and providing opportunities for various perspectives. As he continued to campaign for diversity in the arts, his legacy inspired a new generation to speak their tales authentically and fearlessly.

The Power of Storytelling

At the heart of James Earl Jones' impact is a profound knowledge of the power of storytelling. He understands that stories affect our views, challenge cultural standards, and bring us together on a fundamental level. Whether through theater or film, he constantly advocated for stories that reflect the intricacies of the human experience.

Engaging With Social Issues

Jones' art frequently addresses current societal concerns, encouraging viewers to consider their ideas and ideals. He encourages audiences to engage in meaningful discourse about the world around them by portraying characters that face bigotry, injustice, and personal struggle. This devotion to social consciousness ensures that his legacy will be remembered as a catalyst for change rather than merely entertainment.

A Voice That Will Echo Forever

As we come to the end of our journey through James Earl Jones' incredible life, it is evident that his voice has changed generations—not just in film and theater, but in society as a whole. His achievements have had a lasting impact on the arts, inspiring many people to embrace their creativity and pursue their hobbies.

The Enduring Influence

Even as he walks away from the spotlight, his voice will live on through new projects and adaptations for years to come. Young actors will study his performances, directors will be inspired by his approach to character development, and audiences will continue to find comfort in the wisdom inherent in his words.

A Lasting Legacy

James Earl Jones' impact goes beyond accolades and awards; it demonstrates the transformational power of art. His journey served as a reminder that narrative is an essential component of our humanity, allowing us to comprehend ourselves and one another.

In honoring James Earl Jones, we honor a voice that has changed generations and will be recognized as one of the most important in the history of film and theater. As we move forward into an ever-changing landscape of storytelling, let us take with us the lessons learned from this incredible artist: embrace our tales, elevate various voices, and strive for authenticity in every narrative we tell.

www.ingramcontent.com/pod-product-compliance
Lightning Source LLC
Chambersburg PA
CBHW021347160726
47994CB00007B/2873